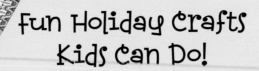
Fun Holiday Crafts
Kids Can Do!

Cinco de Mayo Crafts

Carol Gnojewski

Enslow Elementary
an imprint of
Enslow Publishers, Inc.

40 Industrial Road   PO Box 38
Box 398   Aldershot
Berkeley Heights, NJ 07922   Hants GU12 6BP
USA   UK

http://www.enslow.com

Enslow Elementary, an imprint of Enslow Publishers, Inc.

Enslow Elementary® is a registered trademark of Enslow Publishers, Inc.

Library of Congress Cataloging-in-Publication Data

Gnojewski, Carol.
    Cinco de Mayo crafts / Carol Gnojewski.—1st ed.
        p. cm. — (Fun holiday crafts kids can do)
    Includes bibliographical references and index.
    ISBN 0-7660-2344-3
    1. Holiday decorations—Juvenile literature. 2. Handicraft—Juvenile literature.
3. Cinco de Mayo (Mexican holiday)—Juvenile literature. I. Title. II. Series.
TT900.H6G5897 2004
745.594'162—dc22   2004009624

Printed in the United States of America

10 9 8 7 6 5 4 3 2 1

To Our Readers: We have done our best to make sure all Internet Addresses in this
book were active and appropriate when we went to press. However, the author and the
publisher have no control over and assume no liability for the material available on those
Internet sites or on other Web sites they may link to. Any comments or suggestions can
be sent by e-mail to comments@enslow.com or to the address on the back cover.

Illustration credits: Crafts prepared by June Ponte. © 1999 Artville, LLC., p. 4.
Photography by Carl Feryok.

Cover Illustration: Carl Feryok

Contents

Safety Note: Be sure to ask for help from an adult, if needed, to complete these crafts!

introduction

Cinco de Mayo means the fifth of May. It is the date of a hard-won battle in North America. The battle took place in 1862 in the state of Puebla, in central Mexico. Townspeople and Mexicans fought along with Mexican troops. Together, they defended the city of Puebla against an attacking French army. The French were marching to nearby Mexico City, the capital of Mexico. They wanted to take control of the country. The Mexican victory proved that Mexicans would unite to protect their freedom. At this time, Benito Juárez was the president of Mexico. Later that year, he

made Cinco de Mayo a holiday called *Batalla de Puebla*. This means Battle of Puebla. Today, it is not a national holiday in Mexico. But it is remembered with *fiestas,* or parties, in Puebla and other regions of the country. In the United States, Cinco de Mayo is a day when Mexican Americans show pride in their heritage. Parades, arts festivals, and rodeos are some of the ways it is celebrated.

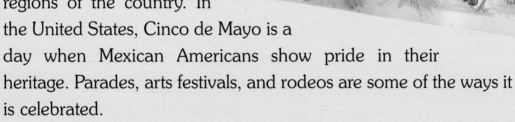

Word Balloons

Street vendors sell goods year-round at the zócalo (SOH-cah-low), or town square. Helium balloon vendors are popular during holidays such as Cinco de Mayo. Some vendors sell balloons with drawings and greetings written in Spanish. Spanish is Mexico's national language. Surprise a friend with a cheery Word Balloon.

What You Will Need:

- balloons
- permanent markers
- yarn or ribbon

1. Blow up the balloons and tie them. Or you can leave them deflated.

2. Use permanent markers to write holiday phrases on the balloons. Some phrases are listed below.

3. Tie yarn or ribbon around the knot at the end of each balloon. Phrases and designs will enlarge if you write or draw before you inflate the balloon.

Alegría (ah-lay-GREE-ah)—Happiness

Amigo (ah-MEE-go)—Friend

¡Buen dia! (boo-ayn DEE-ah)—Good day!

Celebración (cel-ah-BRAH-see-own)—Celebration

Cinco de Mayo (SIN-coh day MY-oh)—5th of May

¡Fiesta! (fee-ES-ta)—Party!

Hola (OH-la)—Hello

¡Ole! (Oh-LAY)—Bravo!

Gather up your supplies . . .

Blow up the balloon and tie it off . . .

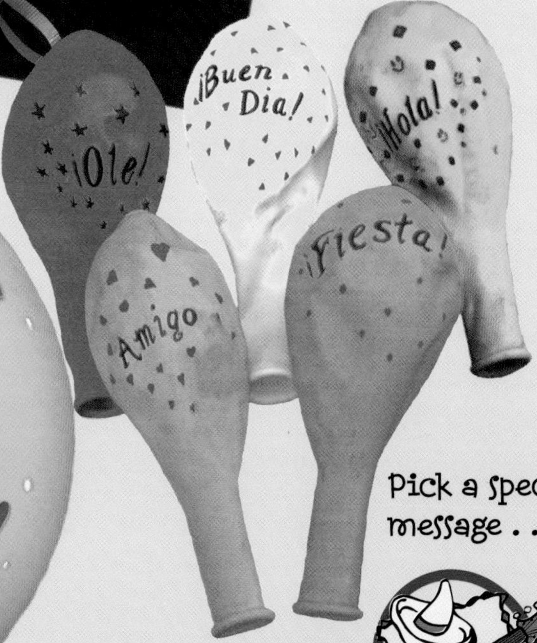

AMIGO

¡Ole!

¡Buen Dia!

¡Hola!

Amigo

¡Fiesta!

Pick a special message . . .

your balloon is ready for display!

Holiday Hint:
Bundle balloons and hand them out to friends.

Peace Votive

Many Mexicans display special candles in their homes. People light them for luck, protection, and prayer. On Cinco de Mayo, create your own Peace Votive. **Have an adult light it for you.**

What You Will Need:

- glass jar
- tempera paint or paint pens
- paintbrushes
- black marker

- felt
- scissors
- white glue or rubber cement
- green, white, or red pillar candle

- bandana or placemat (optional)
- fresh or dried flowers (optional)

1. Thoroughly clean and dry a tall, narrow glass jar, such as a jam or an olive jar.

2. With paint pens or tempera paint and paintbrushes, draw designs on the outside of the jar. See page 26 for peace symbols and symbols of Mexico.

3. When the paint is dry, trace the bottom of the jar onto a piece of felt with a black marker.

4. Use scissors to cut out the felt circle you have traced. Glue the felt circle to the bottom of the jar.

5. Place a green, white, or red candle inside the jar.

6. If you wish, spread a bandana or a placemat in the center of a flat surface in your home, such as a table or a shelf.

7. Set the Peace Votive on top of the bandana or placemat.

8. Arrange fresh or dried flowers around the candle. **Ask an adult to light the candle for you.**

Trace the felt for the bottom . . .

Glue it onto the candle holder . . .

Your painted jar is finished and the candle is ready to be lighted.

Holiday Hint:

Make a wish for world peace and unity.

Border Blooms

Brightly colored paper flowers decorate parade floats and dancers' costumes on Cinco de Mayo. These coffee filter blooms are stronger than tissue paper. They are designed to look like dahlias, Mexico's national flower.

What You Will Need:

- coffee filters
- food dye
- vinegar
- bowls
- water
- herbs (optional)
- essential oils (optional)
- newspaper
- scissors
- hole punch
- pipe cleaners

1. Spread newspaper to protect your workspace. Fill bowls with 1 cup of water and 1 tablespoon of vinegar. Add several drops of food dye into each bowl. Make sure to use only one color of food dye per bowl. If you wish, add to the water sweet-smelling herbs such as rosemary and cloves. Or mix in a few drops of essential oils for fragrance.

2. Dip each coffee filter into the dyed water until it has absorbed the color.

3. Squeeze the excess water out of each filter. Then smooth the filter so that it lies flat. Let it dry on the newspapers.

4. When the colored filters are dry, use craft scissors to scallop the edges. Or cut the edges into rounded triangles.

5. Stack three or more filters on top of each other. Punch two holes in the center of the stack of filters. Be sure to punch the holes close together.

6. Thread the pipe cleaners up one set of holes and down the other. Twist the ends of the stems together.

7. Fluff the filters up toward the center.

Start with the food dye . . .

Dip the coffee filter in the dye . . .

Assemble the layers . . .

Make a bunch to create a colorful bouquet!

Holiday Hint:
Use the blooms to decorate your home or your hair.

Sombrero Visor

A sombrero (sum-BRAY-roh) is a large, Mexican hat with a wide brim. Sombrero comes from the word sombra, or "shade." Most sombreros are made of straw or felt. Some are decorated with pom-poms and fancy trim. Charros (char-rose), or Mexican cowboys, wear sombreros to shade their heads from the hot Mexican sun.

What You Will Need:

- large brown paper bag
- scissors
- crayons or markers
- ruler
- glue (optional)
- fabric trim or ribbons (optional)

1. Use scissors to cut open a large brown paper bag. Spread the grocery paper flat.

2. Draw a large oval on the paper at least 6 inches wider than your head. Use scissors to cut out the large oval. In the center of the oval, trace a circle the size of your head.

3. Use scissors to cut the circle out of the center of the sack.

4. Fold the outer edges of the oval upward. This is the hat brim or visor.

5. Draw designs along the edges of the brim. Or glue on fabric trim or ribbons.

6. Punch holes and string beads at the bottom of the brim, if you wish.

Start with a
paper bag . . .

Draw a circle in the
center and cut it
out . . .

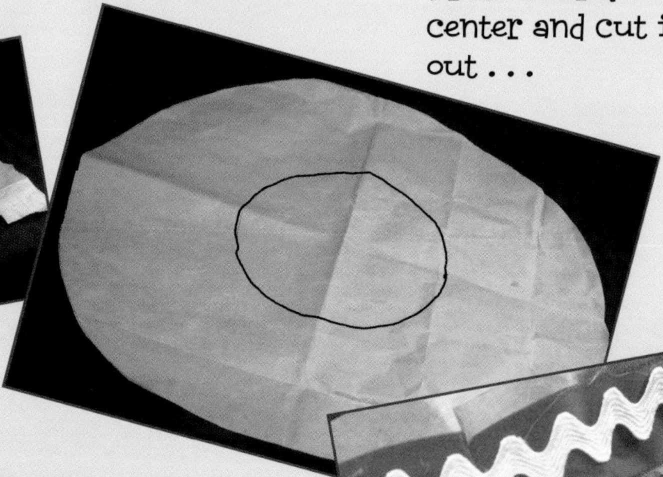

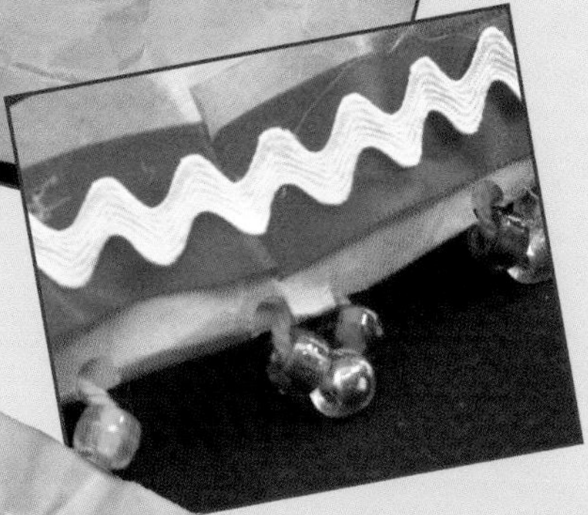

If you wish,
decorate
with beads
and trim . . .

Your sombrero
visor is ready to
wear!

Holiday Hint:

Set the Sombrero Visor on
your head. Your head
becomes the crown of the
hat. You are ready to
participate in a fiesta. ¡Ole!

Cinco de Mayo Messages

Mexico City is home to the first printing press in North America. It was built in 1539. President Benito Juárez believed in books and education. He grew up in a village without a school. He was a teenager before he learned to read and write Spanish.

What You Will Need:

- scrap paper
- plastic foam paper plates
- scissors
- pencils
- red or green tempera paint
- white construction paper

1. Use the scrap paper to develop a message or a design that you wish to print. If you want, use the pattern on page 27 to get started.

2. Cut the flat center out of the foam plate. This will be your printing template.

3. Use a pencil to draw or write your message or design on the foam. Keep in mind that all words and designs will print backwards. To print the word "fiesta" you will need to spell it "atseif." Now dip your paintbrush in red or green tempera paint. Paint over your design or message. Do this lightly so that the paint will not reach the pencil grooves.

4. Press the plate paint side down onto a piece of white paper. Remove it to reveal your message.

Write your message
on some paper . . .

Trace onto a
foam plate . . .

Press the plate with
paint onto a colored
piece of paper . . .

Decorate with
festive colors!

Holiday Hint:

Make many Cinco de Mayo
messages to hand out to your
family and friends.

Paper Poncho

Mexicans in Puebla and other regions wear homemade fabric ponchos instead of jackets. Ponchos are woven like blankets. They have a hole in the center for the head to slip through. Poncho designs are very colorful and unique. The style of weaving can help to tell where in Mexico it was made.

What You Will Need:

- poster board
- scissors
- glue

- ruler (optional)
- yarn

1. Fold the poster board in half from short end to short end. Use scissors to cut a semicircular hole along the fold. This is the neck hole. Make it just big enough to slip your head through.

2. Cut yarn into lengths. The pieces should be longer than each half of the poster board.

3. Set the poster board on a smooth surface. Refold. Spread lines of glue from the top of the neck fold to the bottom of the poster board. Space lines evenly, about ½-inch apart. Use a ruler if necessary. Work on one half of the poncho at a time.

4. One at a time, press the yarn lengths into the lines of glue. They will hang off of the bottom of the poster board. This is the fringe.

5. Trim the fringe so that it falls evenly.

6. Repeat steps 4 through 6 on the other side of the Paper Poncho.

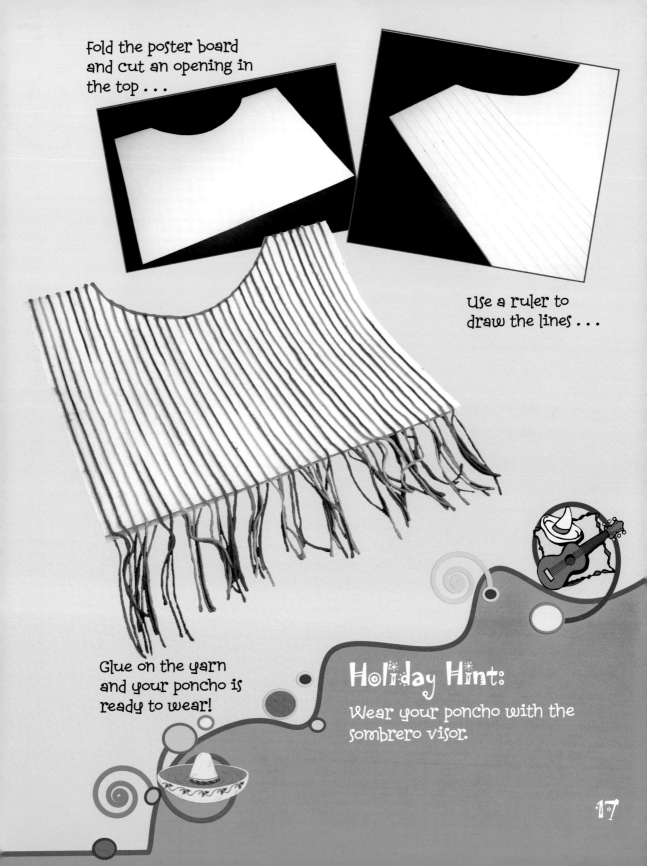

Fold the poster board and cut an opening in the top . . .

Use a ruler to draw the lines . . .

Glue on the yarn and your poncho is ready to wear!

Holiday Hint:

Wear your poncho with the sombrero visor.

Cinco de Mayo Flag Chain

Mexico's national colors are red, green, and white. These are the colors of the Mexican flag. The green bar stands for independence. White means religion. Red is for unity.

What You Will Need:

- green, white, and red construction paper
- ruler
- scissors
- tape
- small circular labels
- green and red markers
- red, white, or green streamers (optional)

1. Cut green, white, and red construction paper into 1-inch by 6-inch strips.

2. Begin with a green strip. Tape the ends together to form a circle.

3. Thread a white strip through the green circle. Tape the ends together.

4. Then thread a red strip through the white circle. Tape the ends together. Continue this pattern to form a green, white, and red paper chain.

5. Divide the circular labels into three bars. Color the first bar green. Color the last bar red. Leave the middle one white.

6. Stick the colored circles on the paper chain.

7. If you wish, divide streamers into equal 4-inch lengths. Cut slits into the bottom of each streamer to make fringe.

8. Use the colored circles to attach the streamers to the chain.

Cut pieces of construction paper and streamers . . .

Make the links of the chain . . .

Color in the labels . . .

Stick the colored stickers onto the chain . . .

Your flag chain is ready to decorate your room!

Holiday Hint:

Make your Cinco de Mayo Flag Chain as long as you wish. Hang it across rooms, doors, and windows.

Feather Mosaic Shield

Fifty different kinds of hummingbirds make their home in Mexico. Ancient Mexican people named cities and buildings after them. The feathers of hummingbirds and other beautiful birds were traded like money. Feathers were woven into fans, headdresses, clothes, and headbands. Mexicans still wear these items during ceremonies and fiestas.

What You Will Need:

- scissors
- poster board
- craft feathers
- markers or crayons
- glitter
- glue
- construction paper
- tape

1. Use scissors to cut the poster board into an oval or shield shape.

2. Arrange feathers on the shield. Make patterns or overlap feathers. Try to vary the size and color of feathers you use.

3. Glue feathers to the poster board. Draw designs around the edges of the shield with markers or crayons.

4. If you wish, squirt glue on the feathers and designs. Sprinkle glitter over the glue.

5. Cut an 8-inch by 2-inch rectangle out of construction paper. Place a piece of tape at both ends of the rectangle.

6. Tape the ends of the rectangle to the back of the shield. The middle of the rectangle will not be taped. This is the handle of the shield.

Cut the shield shape . . .

Add feathers . . .

Decorate the edges
and glue the handle
on the back. . .

Your shield is ready to
show your family and
friends!

Holiday Hint:
Use green, white, and red
feathers for more holiday
flair.

21

Mexican Mayo Mural

Since ancient times, Mexicans have painted murals on walls and ceilings of homes, buildings, churches, and temples. Famous murals such as those painted by the artist Diego Rivera show scenes that tell stories of the history of Mexico. Cinco de Mayo is the fifth day of the fifth month in our calendar year.

What You Will Need:

- poster board or butcher paper
- masking tape
- books about Mexico
- scrap paper
- markers or crayons
- tempera paint and paintbrushes (optional)

1. On scrap paper, brainstorm a list of at least five things you can find in Mexico. A sample list might be flowers, birds, volcanoes, pyramids, and ears of corn. If you want, use the patterns on pages 28 and 29 to get started.

2. Ask permission to tape the poster board or paper to a wall or door in your home.

3. Write the number five in the center of the paper.

4. Using markers or crayons, draw five items from you list on the poster board or paper. If you wish, you can use tempera paint to paint your mural.

Gather up your supplies . . .

Brainstorm five objects that are in Mexico . . .

Put your mural together and add bright colors!

Holiday Hint:

Laminate your murals to make festive placemats.

Sun Stone Sun Prints

The sun was all-important to ancient Mexican peoples. Aztec Indians who lived where Mexico City and Puebla are today built pyramids and monuments to the sun. The Aztec sun stone is an enormous stone sculpture shaped like the sun. The stone disk weighs 79 tons! It was used as a calendar. Pictures called glyphs carved in the stone stood for different days of the month. Build your own sun sculpture and let the sun print it for you.

What You Will Need:

- dark colored construction paper
- rock
- items of various shapes (toys, blocks, sticks, odds and ends)
- markers (optional)
- stickers (optional)

1. Place a large rock in the center of a piece of dark colored construction paper.

2. Arrange various odds and ends around the rock to create a sculpture in the shape of the sun.

3. Set the sculpture and paper out in the sun. This may take several hours. Be patient.

4. Let the sun bleach the exposed paper.

5. Remove the sculpture from the paper to reveal your Sun Stone Print. If you wish, decorate the print with stickers and markers.

Place a large rock in the center of the paper . . .

Set the sculpture out in the sun . . .

By the end of the day, your sun print will be done!

Holiday Hint:

For the best results, be sure to wait for a bright, sunny day.

Patterns

Use tracing paper to copy the patterns on these pages. Ask an adult to help you cut and trace the shapes onto contruction paper.

For the Peace Votive:

Peace Symbols:
Dove
Peace action symbol
Interlocking circles
Rainbows
V for victory
Hands
Olive branches

Mexican Symbols:
Sun
Mexican flag
Mexican Emblem—eagle eating a snake while perched on a cactus
Roses
Dahlias—national flower

At 100%

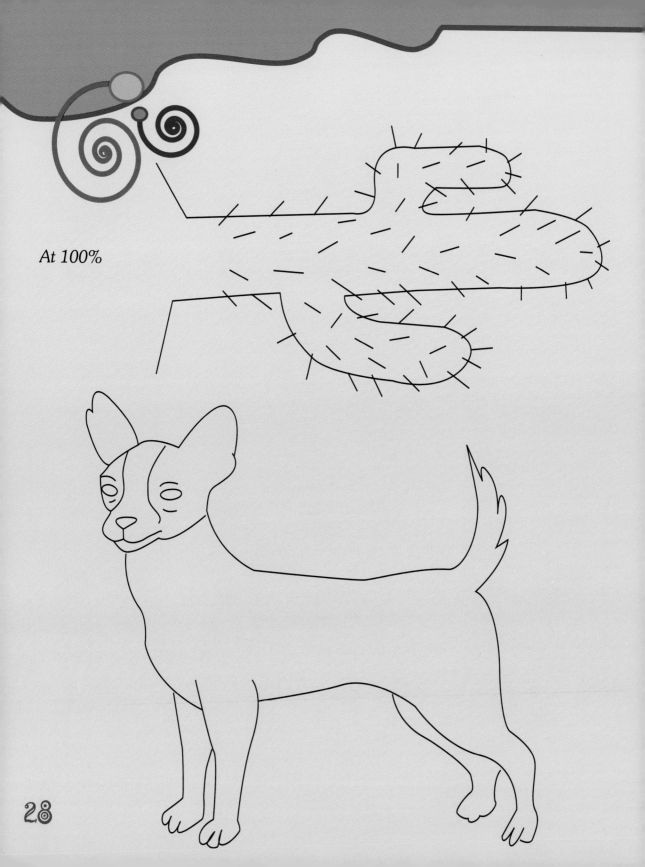

At 100%

At 100%

Reading About Cinco de Mayo

Ancona, George. *The Fiestas*. New York: Benchmark Books, 2002.

DeAngelis, Gina. *Mexico*. Mankato, Minn.: Blue Earth Books, 2003.

Garcia, James. *Cinco de Mayo: A Mexican Holiday About Unity and Pride*. Chanhassen, Minn.: Child's World, 2003.

Gnojewski, Carol. *Cinco de Mayo: Celebrating Hispanic Pride*. Berkeley Heights, N.J.: Enslow Publishers, Inc., 2002.

Wade, Mary Dodson. *Cinco de Mayo*. New York: Children's Press, 2003.

Internet Addresses

Cinco de Mayo Celebration

Find all kinds of information from this Kids Domain site.

<http://www.kidsdomain.com/holiday/cinco>

México for Kids

Learn more about Mexico.

<http://www.elbalero.gob.mx/index_kids.html>

Index